MW00682068

DISCOVER THE MESSAGES

IN YOUR DREAMS

WITH THE ULLMAN METHOD

What People Are Saying

Janet Wahl has written a reader-friendly instruction guide for the celebrated Dream Appreciation method created by Dr. Montague Ullman several years ago. Orthodox psychoanalysts would be shocked at this method because it puts the dreamer in control of the process and even assumes that dreamers are the best interpreters of their own dreams. However, the Ullman method has built-in safeguards as well as step-by-step instructions that empower the group members as well as the dreamer. Janet Wahl has performed a great service to dreamers everywhere by writing this book as well as to the memory of Dr. Ullman, the brilliant psychoanalyst who developed, practiced, and taught it.

— *Stanley Krippner, PhD, Alan W. Watts Professor of Psychology, Saybrook University. Co-author,* Dream Telepathy; *Co-editor,* Perchance to Dream

Janet S. Wahl, the author of *Discover the Messages in Your Dreams with the Ullman Method,* shares with her reader the fruits of her long and intimate apprenticeship under Montague Ullman, MD, beyond doubt the greatest dream psychiatrist in modern times. Using an actual dream and an actual dreamer, she familiarizes the reader with the easy steps of Ullman's revolutionary group approach for making sense of dreams. This method recognizes that you and I—and not Freud, Jung, any of their theories, or the theories or

ideas of their students—are the only authorities on the meaning of
our own dreams. Our dreams are their own theory of who we are
at the time we dreamed them. Wahl offers a wonderful explanation
for why a group of ordinary people, without any specific medical or
psychotherapy training, can be so effective in helping a dreamer to
decipher her dream. It turns out, as the quantum physicists tell us,
we are not at all actually the separate entities we take ourselves to
be. We are connected in important, deep ways. The dream of any
one of us touches us all in such profound and interesting ways that
we are potentiated to spawn a flurry of notions that, whether right
or wrong, prove capable of catapulting the dreamer into a sudden
understanding of the meaning of her dream. Every dream makes
sense. Every dream brings us closer to who we really are, so every
dream empowers us. Here is one new book that will make a real
difference in your life.

— *William R. Stimson, PhD, Founder of Ullman Experiential Dream Groups Worldwide*

Janet Wahl's step-by-step approach to the Ullman method is crafted
in such a way that the dream work process becomes accessible to
all. *Discover the Messages in Your Dreams with the Ullman Method*
serves as a manual for those new to dream working as well as offering
a review for the experienced Ullman method practitioner. She uses
many real-life examples from dream groups she has led, which makes
the method come alive for the reader. Wahl also offers a quick, easy-
to-use reference chart as a guide for following the Ullman process.
For those of us who knew Monte Ullman, Wahl extends a special
treat. She presents personal experiences about Ullman's life that he
shared with her. These wonderful, engaging personal stories are being
offered for the first time in print. This is a book that belongs on every

dream worker's book shelf. For those who would like to know more about working with dreams, it is an invaluable tool.

— *Jacquie Lewis, PhD, Co-Director of the Dream Studies Certificate Program, Saybrook University. Co-Editor,* WORKING WITH DREAMS AND PTSD NIGHTMARES *and* WEAVING DREAMS INTO THE CLASSROOM; *Chapter Author,* PERCHANCE TO DREAM

Discover the Messages in Your Dreams with the Ullman Method by Janet Wahl provides a comprehensive, step-by-step tutorial of Dr. Montague Ullman's Experiential Dream Group Method. Every aspect of this process, which is practiced globally, is clearly delineated for dream group leaders, beginners and professionals alike. Its many examples familiarize the reader with the tone and structure embedded in the process. Janet Wahl, a devoted Ullman practitioner and ThetaHealing Master, has skillfully woven the Ullman philosophy into this book, emphasizing trust and privacy for the dreamer throughout. It concludes with insights into the mind of a man who early-on recognized that the dream when shared with a group reveals our interconnectedness to each other and the world around us. This is a reminder that we are members of a single species, Ullman's legacy to group dream work.

— *Judy B. Gardiner, Author of* LAVENDER: AN ENTWINED ADVENTURE IN SCIENCE AND SPIRIT

Discover the
MESSAGES IN YOUR
Dreams
WITH THE
ULLMAN METHOD

JANET S. WAHL

MINDBALANCE LLC

Published by MindBalance LLC
Albuquerque, NM 87120
www.mindbalance.us
© 2015 by Janet S. Wahl

All rights reserved. No part of this publication may be reproduced, stored in a retrieval system, or transmitted, in any form or by any means, electronic, mechanical, photocopying, recording, or otherwise, without the prior permission of the publisher.

Printed in the United States of America

ISBN (Kindle): 978-09963346-1-7
ISBN (paperback): 978-0-9963346-0-0

All comments in the dream group are from actual people. Names have been changed to protect the privacy and safety of the dreamer. Any resemblance to actual persons, living or dead, is entirely coincidental.

ThetaHealing® is a registered trademark of Vianna Stibal, ThetaHealing Institute of Knowledge.

The information in this book is intended for educational purposes only. No content in this book is to serve as medical or psychological advice. It is not therapy. Please contact a medical professional immediately for any condition that requires a diagnosis or medical or psychological attention. The author disclaims any liability arising directly or indirectly from all of the practices in this book. In the event you use any of the information in this book for yourself or others, which is your constitutional right, the author and publisher assume no responsibility for your actions.

Library of Congress Control Number: 2015908273

Cover design: Scarlett Rugers
Editor: Holly T. Monteith

Dream Group Process Chart: contributed by Judy B. Gardiner

For Monte

Contents

Foreword xiii

Preface xvii

Acknowledgments.. xix

Introduction 1

1 Dreamer Safety 3

2 The Steps of the Process 7

3 Challenges to Newcomers... 17

4 Listening and Questioning.. 19

5 Orchestration Skills 23

6 Why Does This Work? We Are All Connected 25

7 Functions of Dreams 29

8 The Biology of Dreams 31

9 A Memory of Monte.. 33

Appendix: Dream Group Process... 37

Notes 39

Bibliography... 41

About the Author 43

Foreword

Montague Ullman, MD, has frequently been called the Father of Group Dream Work, and rightfully so. He was helping psychoanalytic candidates learn how to work with dreams when the need for a process to help dreamers not undergoing psychoanalysis became apparent to him. He further realized that the safety of the dreamer had to be a primary consideration for group dream work.

Discover the Messages in Your Dreams with the Ullman Method is a valuable and user-friendly contribution for all those who want to do dream work that protects the safety of dreamers and their process of discovery. But first, some background on how Janet and I arrived at that appreciation.

I met Janet at a dream workshop at a beautiful retreat setting in suburban Philadelphia in the mid-1990s. We were both avid dreamers and dream workers and were attending the workshop to find locally those who shared our interests. We had never met before, but an event at the workshop soon forged a bond that grew into a deep respect and long-term friendship.

Participants were asked who wanted to share a dream, and someone volunteered. This was standard for such workshops. But what happened next took us by surprise. The workshop facilitator had participants ask the dreamer questions—but allowed them to ask directive and invasive questions, which were obviously upsetting to the dreamer. We were both horrified. I believe Janet was the first one to question this approach, and in the ensuing discussion we supported each other because it turned out we had both studied with Montague Ullman.

I remember talking in the parking lot after the workshop and sharing our experiences with Monte in his Leadership Training Workshops. What a different experience they had been! They honored the safety of the dreamer, and they nurtured the dreamer's ability to discover the meaning of her own dream. His groups were completely focused on the dreamer—not any member or the leader's prowess in "interpreting" a dream. That workshop, as disconcerting as it was for both of us, reminded us of the importance of integrity in dream work, including groups conducted by lay dream workers. That had been Monte's intent—to develop a safe process so that everyday people could have access to dream work, even if they weren't in psychoanalysis or psychotherapy. It reminded me of how I was forced to confront my dream values and the path to discovering Monte's process.

It was about a decade earlier, in the 1980s, when I heard about a dream workshop in New Jersey and eagerly signed up. The first part of the workshop was basic information about dreams, which I already knew from all the reading I had done. Right before the break, the facilitator said, "And people can write their names on a slip of paper and put them in this jar, and when we come back, I will pick someone and interpret their dream." That made me uncomfortable, but I wanted to see what happened. The name selected was the woman sitting behind me. She shared her dream, and the facilitator interpreted it. She responded that what he said didn't *feel* right. And he responded that what he had said was what it meant. Ouch! I could feel the woman's discomfort emanating from her.

This man was holding a series of workshops in which I had eagerly anticipated before the session had started. Now I was not so sure. He called me a few weeks later because I had not signed up for his next workshop. This was a crossroads where I had to decide whether or not I was going to stand up for what I believed about working with dreams. I had to be honest and told him why I could not support his method of dream work. I never heard from him again.

Shortly thereafter, I stumbled across Monte and Stan Krippner's book *Dream Telepathy*. Having had precognitive dreams since childhood, I resonated with their work. I can't recall how I connected with Monte in person, but I knew I had found a way to work with dreams that resonated with my values—a way that would encourage and respect the dreamer but not dictate to the dreamer.

The dreamer is the best person to interpret his dream. Period and exclamation point! Monte has said that group members can be midwives to the dream, but it is not their dream.

After leading dream groups for many years, I have repeatedly heard about the pain and damage caused by authority figures of one stripe or another who have told people what their dreams meant—which was different from what they meant to the dreamers. That is what Monte, even as a psychoanalyst, wanted to avoid. That's why the safety and trust he built into his process are so important.

Discover the Messages in Your Dreams with the Ullman Method captures the incontrovertible, fundamental concepts of Monte's process. For seven years (1996–2002) I edited and published *Dream Appreciation,* a newsletter where Monte was able to free himself from the constraints of academic publishing protocol and share his innermost thoughts, feelings, and insights about dreams. However, always the professional, in 1996 he published *Appreciating Dreams,* capturing in great detail how his process works and how dream workers can follow it. In this book, *Discover the Messages in Your Dreams with the Ullman Method,* Janet Wahl tackles Monte's extremely comprehensive process and distills his concepts into thorough yet user-friendly techniques that dream workers can embrace and apply.

Monte's process usually takes at least ninety minutes or more. It is the length of that time that allows dreamers to slowly unravel and reflect on the significance of a dream and gives his process such depth and power. Many groups are not able to dedicate that much time to a single dream. As a result, many people truncate the process but still call it the Ullman process. Unless all the stages are followed, it is not the Ullman process and should never be referred to as such.

Janet Wahl's book is an important contribution to those who care about the integrity of the dream group process, and especially all those who have experienced—or wish they had experienced—Monte's group work. Readers can not only develop a thorough understanding of each stage of Monte's process but also understand the challenges and common mistakes people make at each stage. It is a worthwhile read for everyone who cares about dream work.

Wendy Pannier
Past President, International Association for the Study of Dreams
Editor and publisher of *Dream Appreciation*

Preface

Why would I write about the Experiential Dream Group process? After all, hundreds of books have been written about dreams and their meanings. Furthermore, the founder of this process, Montague Ullman, popularly known as Monte (1916–2008), published many books and articles about the subject, located on a commemorative website (http://siivola.org/monte). Why would I attempt to reiterate less eloquently than he? The answer is twofold. First, many dream workers claim to employ the Ullman process but use only parts of the process. From my perspective, shortened versions shortchange the dreamer. If the group does not complete all the steps of the process, it is not truly an Ullman Dream Group. It may be inspired by Ullman, but it should be called a derivative. Monte[1] made it very clear during his life that if his name is used, the group must follow all the steps. Second, I want to enable more people to utilize his work. I was a member of Montague Ullman's dream groups for more than fifteen years during my career in education as a teacher, professor, and administrator. He convinced me to take his leadership training workshops. The positive impact his method of dream work had on my life was and continues to be enormous. The details of my personal benefits can be found in *Discover the Hidden Beliefs in Your Dreams*. For these reasons, I write this short guide to help others reap the rewards of the complete Ullman process.

Acknowledgments

Several groups of people made this book possible: ThetaHealers, dreamers, and writers. Each group was essential.

My ThetaHealing friends and colleagues were amazed that dream work enhanced their practice. Deborah Steg, Jenna Hiott, Linda Garcia, Dave, and Eric provided impetus and encouraged me along the way. Mona Ruark's feedback on clarity was essential for effectively teaching and leading dream groups.

My dream group friends ensured the accuracy and completeness of the guide. Judy B. Gardiner, familiar with Monte Ullman's work, carries his torch. Her suggestions and additions were priceless. Wendy Pannier, former president of the International Association for the Study of Dreams, as well as a personal friend, encouraged me to rejoin the association and present at its 2015 conference. I am indebted to Markku Siivola for his comments on the manuscript and for his website containing all of Monte's published works. Thank heavens his work is all in one place! William Stimson provided a valuable critique of content. My gratitude extends to the long, private list of dream group members who helped me not only with my dreams but also to learn this process.

Knowledge gained from fellow writers was extremely valuable. The Southwest Writers, a group of supportive friends and colleagues, provided writing and publishing expertise. From this organization I found critique groups whose members patiently read my drafts and encouraged me: Barbara, Maria, Marie, Carmen, and Paula carefully critiqued my work. Kristen Eckstein provided webinars and consultation to lead me through the publishing process. My editor, Holly T. Monteith, and cover designer, Scarlett Rugers, supplied publishing expertise. Without this support, this guide would be left in the dark of night.

Introduction

Welcome to the Experiential Dream Group process. You are about to embark on a journey to explore the messages in your nighttime dreams. How many times have you awakened saying, "What was that all about? Why did I have that dream?" You can ask these questions, but only you, the dreamer, have the answer.

"But I am clueless! How am I supposed to figure it out?"

The Experiential Dream Group process, developed by psychiatrist Montague (Monte) Ullman (1916–2008), can help you discover the factors that precipitated the dream and how the dream relates to your waking life. Note that the name of the process is "Experiential Dream Group" because the group members "experience" or imagine the selected dream as their own to offer projections to the dreamer. Some of their projections, which only the individual dreamer can verify, help the dreamer illuminate the dream messages.

PEOPLE NEW TO DREAM WORK

People new to dream work often confuse *projection, interpretation,* and *analysis.* Interpretations and analyses are opinions of listeners who tell the dreamer what the dream means. In this case, the dreamer receives information as a supplicant because interpretations come from the stance of an authority. In contrast, a projection is an offering that comes from the imagination and empathy of a listener who pretends the dream is his own and offers personal reactions: "If it were my dream, . . ." The ideas about the listener's interior life are offered for the dreamer's consideration. Projections say more about the listener than they do about the dreamer. In this situation, the dreamer is in charge; the dreamer may accept or reject the projection. Dreamers are very sensitive to these different attitudes.

"But I don't dream."

"I can't remember my dreams."

To remember your dreams,
- set the intention to recall your dreams as you drift off to sleep.
- put a pen and notebook next to your bed.
- record your dream before you get out of bed; don't worry about spelling or grammar—write what comes to mind.

To facilitate work on the dream later, record in your notebook
- the feelings in the dream.
- the date of the dream.
- the context: make some notes about the previous day's activities, personal encounters, concerns, and feelings.
- a title (optional): sometimes titles readily emerge; other times they don't—titles are not necessary.

Now you are ready to participate in the Experiential Dream process.

1

Dreamer Safety

THE ESSENCE OF DREAMS

Dreams contain highly personal information from the subconscious mind. In the subconscious language of dream images and metaphors, the truth about us emerges from what Monte calls our incorruptible core.[2] The waking mind edits and revises these dream truths to maintain an acceptable social façade. Dreams vanish as the conscious mind attempts to recall them to avoid seeing these truths.

PURPOSE OF A DREAM GROUP

According to Ullman, this group differs from other groups in that this group exists for the benefit of the dreamer, not for the benefit of group members although that is often an outcome. The dream group is not therapy, but the process is healing.

Dream groups help the dreamer uncover these truths, but to do so, trust and safety must be built. Without safety, the dreamer is more reticent to share and explore, thereby impeding the healing dreams can offer. That's why the dreamer is in charge; the dreamer is the authority for deciphering dream messages.

APPRECIATION, NOT INTERPRETATION

The ethics statement of the International Association for the Study of Dreams (IASD) states very clearly that the dreamer is in charge of the meaning of his dream images. Therefore, rather than the term *dream interpretation,* Monte prefers *dream appreciation,* in the spirit of promoting the dreamer's authority and control.

This guideline ensures the dreamer's psychological safety. The dreamer decides whether to share a dream. She is not obligated because it is "her turn" or because the dreamer "hasn't shared a dream for a long time." The dreamer can stop the process at any time, so before each step, the dreamer is asked, "Do you want to continue?" This guideline ensures the dreamer's psychological safety.

CONFIDENTIALITY

In addition to allowing the dreamer to determine when and what to share, all discussions in the dream group are confidential. What is said in the dream group stays in the dream group. Only the dreamer has the prerogative to discuss his dream outside the group.

No Leading Questions

During the process, leading questions are forbidden. When a group member thinks she knows what the dream means, she may be tempted to ask a question to verify her theory. Instead, the questioner is encouraged to use the stem, "Can you say anything more about . . . ?" For example, the dreamer has shared this dream fragment:

There is a lost dog. It is sitting on my porch at the front door. It looks forlorn.

A group member asks the dreamer, "Can you say anything more about the dog?"

"It looked cold and wet. It was light brown, collie-like. Maybe it was a young dog but bigger than a puppy." Note the additional information the dreamer is willing to share.

In contrast, a leading question might be, "Have you ever had a stray dog show up on your doorstep?" This question leads the dreamer away from the dream and into a memory search, which may or may not have anything to do with the dream. Listen to the dreamer's response to this leading question.

"Many years ago a black Lab puppy was running around the neighborhood. Although it was cute, we were a little afraid because a neighbor had reported a black dog near his home that turned out to be rabid." Not only did this question push the dreamer offtrack, but it also set her wondering if the group member knew something about her dream that she doesn't know or isn't allowed to determine.

So begin the question with the stem, "Can you say anything more about . . . ?" or "Do you want to say anything more about . . . ?" Then the dreamer has a choice whether to share more. The dreamer can, if she wishes, stop the process and preserve privacy. This choice helps to build trust. The more trust that develops among group members, the more willing they are to share and explore dreams.

Let's follow a dream through the stages of the complete Ullman process. An outline of these stages is located in the appendix. This in-depth group sharing method can require one and a half to two hours per dream.

Participants are asked to bring one copy of an unedited dream they'd like to share. A recent dream is preferable, but an older dream is acceptable. At the beginning of the dream group, participants who wish to share a dream agree among themselves as to who has the most pressing need. If no agreement is reached, a coin is tossed. The dreamers decide; the leader does not decide. Dreamers are in control from the beginning.

2

The Steps of the Process

STAGE I: THE DREAM

Volunteer a Dream

"Who has a dream to share?" the leader asks. No one comes forward. Finally, Marilyn, a Japanese-American aerial ballet artist, states, "I have a dream, but it is not recent and only a fragment."

In this case, only one person offers to share. She apologizes that it is only a fragment. "Even fragments hold meanings unknown to the dreamer's conscious mind. There is no such thing as an unimportant dream," the leader states. "When did you have this dream?"

"I can't remember. About a week ago, I guess."

"Tell us your dream slowly, so we can write it down." Recording the dream allows two things: (1) the emotion and nonverbal cues of the dreamer may become apparent and (2) the group can refer to details of the dream during the process. Marilyn recounts the dream as the participants record it:

> *I am at a study group. I am not told something.*
> *I get very angry. Mom and Auntie Mary are there.*
> *I yell at them for being gone.*

Clarifying Questions

After all have recorded the dream, they ask clarifying questions:

- Who in the dream is real in waking life?

- Is the place real?

- Are Mom and Auntie their respective ages today?
- What are your feelings in the dream (not feelings about the dream after waking)?

Marilyn responds, "The study group is my craniosacral study group. Mom is my mother; Auntie Mary is her sister. It's a living room in a house in the suburbs, not real in waking life. My yelling is telling them they should not have left. They left with a small group of people and then returned."

"Are there feelings in the dream?"

"I felt betrayed and angry." The group now has facts about the dream. Note that the dreamer has not divulged her interpretations about the dream or the feelings she had about the dream after waking.

STAGE II: THE GAME

Feelings

The "Game" is the time devoted to group projections. Members imagine the dream as their own to evoke the feelings they would have had. Sharing their personal feelings may stimulate the dreamer to make more associations. Group members are not giving interpretations but only their personal feelings as if the dream had been theirs. Participants do not look at the dreamer as they share their projections. This allows the dreamer to listen without becoming defensive and interrupting the flow of ideas.

Metaphors

After the group explores and shares feelings with the dreamer, they play with metaphors; they imagine real-life situations that the dream images bring to mind. These are simple projections offered to the dreamer to help find more feelings and possible waking life relationships. The dreamer may accept or reject these projections. He is invited to take notes because sometimes projections resonate days and weeks later. Again, the group members avoid looking at the dreamer.

Let's follow Marilyn's dream using the complete process.

Stage IIA: Feelings—"If it were my dream . . ."

"Do you want to continue, Marilyn?" the leader asks.

"Yes."

"It is now time to make the dream our own. We will talk about the dream as if we had this dream, sharing with each other our feelings and moods that the imagery evokes in us. These are our projections, our offerings for the dreamer to consider. Do not look at the dreamer as you give your projection. 'In my dream, I feel . . .' is a good way to state your projections. Let's start with feelings." Although the instruction is to give feelings first, often the group members can't help themselves and offer metaphors, as happened in this case.

The group responds:

- "In my dream I am the odd man out. I've come to study with good intentions, and all this clandestine communication is going on."

- "I feel isolated."

- "My mom and aunt are well intentioned, but I'm angry. Mom should be on my side. They aren't supportive. I feel abandoned."

- "My family are not behaving themselves."

- "They are a bad reflection on me in my group."

- "Is it because they are there that I haven't been told something?"

- "I feel that my mother will have to change, so she is sabotaging by leaving."

- "There has been a crime committed off-stage which makes me uncomfortable and insecure."

- "Something is not right in my family. Why wasn't I told? I feel disrespected."

- "It's so ironic. Cranial work is based on trust, and this is the opposite of what's supposed to happen in the group."

- "There is a sense of chaos that makes me feel out of control."

- "It does feel good to express my anger; it gets me back to myself."

Stage IIB: Metaphors—"If it were my dream . . ."

"Let's play with the metaphors, the way the images associate with imagined real-life situations. We can continue to express more feelings if they come up. Do not offer interpretations or look at the dreamer," the leader instructs.

- "I am knocking heads with my cranial study group."

- "What are my relatives doing there? They don't take my work seriously."

- "Something is not right—they are messing with my head."

- "The group is my family."

- "I would have liked to leave."

- "They violated my sense of good behavior."

- "Rules hold things together, but my relatives are not following the rules of good behavior."

- "I came to the study group to find out information, but it has been withheld. It gives me the sense of purposelessness."

- "'Auntie Mary' sounds like 'anti-merry,' something working against happiness."

- "'Auntie Mary' sounds like 'anti-marry,' don't get married."

- "Why couldn't the group ignore the people who left?"

- "In my dream, the suburbs represent outside-of-consciousness, a form of isolation. I can't get out, but people can see in."

- "My relatives get to break the rules, but I don't."

Stage III: The Dreamer's Response and Dialogue

Now the dreamer is invited to explore her life for more associations. In Stage IIIA, the dream is "returned" to the dreamer, who is invited to say as much or as little as she wishes without interruption. In Stage IIIB, the context, the day residue, is also explored with the dreamer's permission. The group asks what was going on in waking life at the time of the dream. Context questions can extend to preceding weeks, months, and even years. In the Playback, Stage IIIC, a member reads the dream aloud to the dreamer. Further questions may help to uncover more associations. Before each step, the dreamer is asked if she wants to continue.

Stage IIIA: Dreamer Response

"Do you want to go on? This is your dream; you may stop the process any time."

"Yes, please, let's go on."

"You are invited to say whatever you wish without interruption. Do not share things you are uncomfortable in sharing. We will all listen; just tell us when you are finished," the leader instructs.

Because trust has been established over time, Marilyn shares freely, including information about her dream and life that was unknown to the group. "That was a lot for a couple of sentences' worth of dream! There is a land of mystery here. Why were Mom and Auntie Mary coming into my world? They are getting old and on their way out, dying. The death process asks, 'Where did they go? Why did they leave?' They are supposed to be here. They shouldn't leave. Why didn't they tell me about death?

"It did feel good to express the anger. When I woke, I asked myself, why was I just yelling at them? Can I use my anger more constructively?

"Someone said something about the house in the suburbs where the craniosacral group was meeting. There were rooms in that house that were closed, mysterious. I wasn't being supported there, which made me angry. The group seems to need more support than they can give, which makes me feel isolated. It's the antithesis of the purpose of the group, which is to support. . . . I think that's all I can say."

Note that this information may not make sense to the listening group members; however, it is important that the dreamer is heard and that she has time to make the associations meaningful to her. It is not the group's responsibility to make sense of the dreamer's comments; the dreamer is in charge of making meaning.

Stage IIIB1: The Context—Dialogue

The context of the dreamer's waking life is very likely to show up in a dream. Context, or day residue, includes, but is not limited to,

- activities of the previous days, weeks, or months
- feelings about an event
- feelings when drifting to sleep
- thoughts when drifting to sleep
- phone calls
- books read or media watched
- conversations

These feelings, memories of events, and thoughts reside in the subconscious mind to create dreams.

After receiving permission to continue, the leader asks Marilyn, "What happened the day of the dream?"

"I just can't remember." The group waits in silence as Marilyn searches her memory. "I think I was supposed to rehearse on the trapeze. I didn't. I didn't know how much to push myself. I went to my ballet class. I had clients at night. I rehearsed all week with Jim, a dance partner who wants to perform in the future. I had been rehearsing and was sore in spots that are usually not sore. I felt a little pushed.

"I saw my friend Judy. She lost her father-in-law recently. Another client lost his father.

"In August I usually have a lot of anxiety. It is around loss and death. I just let the sadness come up; it is nonspecific. This year I lost three friends. Oh, in August there is the Obon Ceremony.[3] It is in mid-August, around the 11th or 12th, and lasts for three days. It's a Japanese festival during which families gather and light candles and set them off in little boats to commemorate the people who have died in the past year. There is also Hiroshima Day, August 6 or 7. That anxiety in August—I'm always feeling like I will be attacked from behind and killed.

"I was reading transcripts in Los Angeles. I am in the process of interviewing and recording the stories of family members about their experience in the Japanese internment camps in the U.S. during World War II. Mr. Kobata was shot and killed at the end of July 1942. My grandfather testified at the trial of the guard who shot him. Then my uncle asked me last summer if I knew that Mr. Kobata was shot in camp. Mr. Kobata had suffered TB and could barely breathe in the camp in New Mexico. Another man who was lame was also killed at the same time. My grandfather gave a character witness to indicate that neither man could have run away like they were accused.

"My mother and aunt grew up speaking English, similarly to me. They would never have been to the study group; it's way over their heads. They never said anything about the camps as I was growing up. Now that my aunt is in her senior years, she has talked to school groups about the camps, but she wouldn't have told me. She knows that I am working on a project, but there is no family curiosity about it. It's just too difficult for all of my family members."

Note that Marilyn shares all this information as stated. No questions are asked during these comments. The group has to piece together the information she shares to construct the story. Marilyn states simply and directly everything as it comes to her mind. The number and depth of the associations the dreamer is able to make illustrate the power of the context stage.

Stage IIIB2: Context—The Playback
The leader explains, "During this stage, the members have a chance to ask questions. The only way issues emerge is if we ask questions and search out feelings. If a group member knows something about the dream because she knows the dreamer personally, please write it on a piece of paper and ask the dreamer's permission to share it." With permission to continue, the leader asks, "Who would like to read the dream to Marilyn, scene by scene? Change 'I' to 'you.'"

John volunteers. "You are at a study group. You are not told something."

Marilyn eagerly states, "I was not told about the camps until I was twelve and not about Mr. Kobata until last year. They all knew, but I didn't. I inherited their trauma and have to deal with it without information. It makes me angry."

John continues, "You get very angry. Mom and Auntie Mary are there. You yell at them for being gone."

Marilyn adds, "Why do I have to deal with this? They got out. In the craniosacral work, it is the belief that all cells hold memories. As the egg and sperm hit, all the ancestral energy is transmitted to the embryo. This originates in the concepts of shiatsu and acupuncture. I have been carrying this around all of my life but not having any information about what produced these feelings. I get anxious every August."

Because Marilyn has so thoroughly associated the feelings of anger and betrayal in the dream with the horrors of the internment camps, no further questions are posed. However, had she not been able to do so, questions such as the following may have helped her:

- You don't dream of Auntie Mary and Mom every night. Why do you suppose they showed up in your dream that night?
- Can you say any more about "not being told something"?
- Can you say anything more about the study group?
- Can you say more about "being gone"?

Stage IIIB3: Context—Orchestration

Orchestrations are defined as sharing new ideas about the meaning of the metaphors and feelings in the dream and the contextual information that the dreamer has given. Only new connections are appropriate. This is not the time for interpretations or judgments. It is time for more projections that the dreamer may accept or reject.

"Would you like to see if anyone has orchestrating projections, Marilyn? These will be connections between the content of the dream and what you have already shared but may not have noticed. No one is obligated to share."

"Please continue."

- "For me, this is an important dream. It illuminates your anxiety in August about your family history and the behavior of your relatives, that they withheld information from you. This dream helps you resolve those issues."

- "For me, this dream is about a struggle between anxiety and denial. Your mom's side is in denial and outside of the anxiety, and you've experienced it more directly. This dream relates to the past and grief, which creates a lot of anxiety."

- "How emotionally draining and burdensome! This dream makes a lot come together and, at the same time, is very overwhelming. You are out there alone in terms of your family."

- "You have assumed their burdens. So much you didn't know. The more you learn, the more there is that's unknowable. You only know secondhand. There's the 'uncapturableness' of it all. There's the history and the study, and it's almost like being in two mind-sets at the same time."

- "There is continual accumulation—more grief and pain, in addition to all the deaths."

- "I wonder if you want to know. How did they get through it?"

- "You are innocent until you experience death. Connect and stay connected."

- "It's safer to stay in your head than to know things in other ways."

- "This dream was initially a 'throwaway' dream, one of no significance to you. However, you still remembered it, so it must have signaled to you that it was important. And important it was. It captured your hidden family history in a single scene. Many other people know, but you do not, so you are left without support. Death is a double whammy. Not only do you lose your mother, but you also lose your history and explanations for August anxiety. No wonder you are angry. This little fragment captured something you have struggled with for your entire life. What a beautiful dream! Thanks for sharing it."

Stage IIIB4: Context—The Final Word

The dreamer always has the final word. Marilyn is asked if she cares to respond to the information the dream group has led her to uncover. "If there are any insights or ideas concerning the dream or the work the group did, you are free to share at this time," the leader says to Marilyn.

"I thought this was a little fragment, but it held so much. Thank you," Marilyn states. "I will think more about it."

Stage IV: Delayed Orchestrations

At the next meeting of the dream group, Marilyn will be invited to share any further thoughts she has had about her dream. Members of the group can also share further projections. Dream work is an ongoing process. Dreams, even fragments, are a rich resource to illuminate life.

3

Challenges to Newcomers

The Ullman Dream Group process differs from other group processes in several ways:

- This dream group exists for the benefit of the dreamer. It's not about the participant. Participants do benefit, but the focus is on the dreamer, so participants are not to state how they themselves are benefiting during the group process.

    » For example, if a dream reminds a participant of his own experiences, the participant should not mention this during the group. "That reminds me of my experience . . ." is not appropriate.

    » A way to relate a personal experience to a dream is to state it in this fashion: "If this were my dream, I would . . ." The focus on the dreamer is maintained with an offering the dreamer is free to accept or reject.

- Questions about the dreamer's history are not appropriate.

- It is not therapy. Referrals to the appropriate professionals should be made to the dreamer privately.

- This method can be slow, especially during the steps to find the context, the day residue, and the events that have contributed to the dream images and metaphors. Work on one dream often requires an hour and forty-five minutes to two hours.

Trust among group members creates the success of the group. The more trust there is, the more sharing, the more helpful the projections will be. That is why an ongoing commitment to an Ullman Dream Group is crucial for its success. More safety means more trust and more success.

4

Listening and Questioning

Monte[4] provides some desired qualities of dream group participants that are worthy of reiteration. Good listening and questioning skills are imperative. Questioning the dreamer requires thought, consideration, and highly developed listening skills. Furthermore, the questioners must be guided by what the dreamer says, not by what we as listeners want to know. Considerations are as follows:

- Is the dreamer interested in exploring the question further, or is he inviting us out, that is, wishing to stop the process? If the latter, we do not pursue the question. If the dreamer is inviting us in, we can pursue with open-ended (information-eliciting) questions.

- We avoid leading (information-demanding) questions. A participant may have an unconfirmed interpretation and ask a question to confirm it. As a result, the anxiety level of the dreamer is raised, and she may derail from determining for herself what the image means. For example, I shared the following dream:

A woman was going to pick me up to give me a ride to the school bus. She had rearranged the contents of my purse. I couldn't find my black wallet. I only had the little green one and another item, a huge, oblong purse inside my purse.

I shared what was real in waking life: the black and little green wallets. The huge, oblong purse was not real. All questions should be based only on what I have shared.

A leading question would be, "Have you ever had your wallet stolen?" I never mentioned having had my wallet stolen, so this question throws me offtrack. First, I may not want to share anything about a stolen wallet. Second, this takes my mind off the black wallet and leads me to think about a possible theft. This leading question might have me anxiously respond, "No!" Then I imagine having my wallet stolen, or imagine that the questioner knows something I don't know. This scenario digs a pit in my stomach.

Conversely, an open-ended question—"Can you say anything more about your black wallet?"—invites more information and sticks to the dream.

I respond, "All my membership cards are in my black wallet plus my business bank card and my health insurance cards. The wallet is too large to fit into a pocket, so I don't always take it with me. It has never been stolen. I bought it in New York City the year I left. It's a good wallet, well made. It contains stuff that connects me to society, the world."

See the difference between the response to a leading versus an open-ended question? I volunteered much information about the black wallet from the open-ended question, including a hint about "connecting to society." I could make connections that pertain to me rather than confirming someone else's theory that I had had my wallet stolen.

Another time to ask an appropriate, open-ended question is during the Playback: "You don't always dream of black wallets. Why do you think the black wallet was in your dream that night?" This helps the dreamer relate the image to recent events.

When someone asked me the latter question, it brought to mind another event. "I went to the Flying Star Restaurant and ordered a meal. When it came time to pay, I realized I didn't have my rewards card, which is in my black wallet, so I couldn't accumulate credit toward a free dessert. Sometimes I don't claim something I am entitled to. It is almost as if I am not supposed to take credit for accomplishments. My parents always told me not to brag, but sometimes I get ignored for what I do deserve because I don't speak up for myself. I guess it's like losing a wallet, so to speak."

This open-ended question clearly helped me associate the image with the context of the dream and with one of my life patterns. It is highly doubtful that the question "Have you ever had your wallet stolen?" would have led me to these observations. I would have been distracted, a bit fearful, and gone offtrack.

The participants must help the dreamer explore all the details in the dream, not only the most obvious ones. A question to explore more details might be, "Can you say anything more about 'rearranging' or 'rearranging the contents of your purse'?" Rearranging the contents might not seem so very important compared with the image of missing a wallet. However, consider my response: "I get annoyed when someone messes with my belongings. It feels as if I have given my power to them, letting them decide what is important, what to put in and take out of my purse. Clearly the woman has not only rearranged my power but has also inserted her power as a large, oblong purse, right in the middle of my purse! That's even more annoying."

Now the group elicits more information. I have invited the participants in by revealing my annoyance about having my purse contents rearranged and have gone further to show that this might connect with my perception of my own power. So the question "Can you say anything more about rearranging your power?" is appropriate. If the dreamer has invited us in, the practice of following her yields more relevant information than forwarding individual interpretations. If the dreamer has invited us out, then it is unlikely that she would be receptive to imposed interpretations.

5

Orchestration Skills

During orchestration, participants can offer their own projections of images the dreamer has mentioned that have not been explored. This can be tricky. All the dreamer's responses must be considered and must be given higher priority than the participants' interpretations. If the dreamer has not mentioned a topic, and a group member has an idea, that idea must go unexpressed. Remember, the dreamer is always in control. After all, the dreamer's life experience, not the life experiences of the participants, produced the dream.

Dr. Ullman enumerates the requisite orchestration skills:

1. Listen to everything the dreamer says during the dialogue, not only to her initial responses.

2. Look for relationships between what the dreamer says and the metaphorical possibilities.

3. Learn how to stay with what has emerged from the dreamer. Do not give projections that are unrelated to what the dreamer has said.

4. Look for significant serial relationships between image and context.

5. Learn how to organize the material so that the relationships between the images and context are clarified for the dreamer. This is an orchestration.[5]

Orchestrations vary. Some participants attempt to tell the whole story of the dream and its meaning from beginning to end. This can become tedious and repetitive, unless the orchestration is focused on new ideas. Other participants state in a few sentences the power of the dream. Others may choose not to offer a projection, which is also acceptable. Orchestrations are projections, ideas that the dreamer may accept, think about, or reject. When the contributions are complete, the very last question should be put to the dreamer: "You have the last word. Is there anything you wish to say?" This ends the orchestration step.

Participants often wish to tell the dreamer how his dream relates to their personal experience and how the dream impacts them. Often they attempt to do this during the orchestration. However, the orchestration step is intended to focus only on the dream and the dreamer, not the participants. In Monte's groups, we would refrain from relating our own experiences until we left his house and were in the parking lot. Often we would linger to offer this information to the dreamer. Monte called this the "parking lot" discussion. I have been in groups that mix these offerings. If the intention is to conduct an Ullman dream group, I suggest closing the orchestration and ending the session. If the leader finds it helpful to the dreamer, participants can make statements about themselves after the closing. Once participants begin to talk about themselves, the Ullman process, and possibly also the safety of the dreamer, is compromised.

At the beginning of the next session, the dreamer is asked again if he has had any other thoughts about his dream: a delayed orchestration.

6

Why Does This Work? We Are All Connected

In his telepathic dream studies,[6] Monte found scientific evidence that we are all connected. He also knew that dream group participants connected to another's dream in a profound way. His search for evidence led him to the theories of quantum physicist David Bohm, who

> *believes the reason subatomic particles are able to remain in contact with one another regardless of the distance separating them is not because they are sending some sort of mysterious signal back and forth, but because their separateness is an illusion. Bohm postulates that the ultimate nature of physical reality is not a collection of separate objects (as it appears to us), but rather it is an undivided whole that is in perpetual dynamic flux. For Bohm, the insights of quantum mechanics and relativity theory point to a universe that is undivided and in which all parts merge and unite in one totality.[7]*

So if we are not "separate objects" but rather part of a whole, then we contain elements and feelings of other people. This explains how we can relate intimately to another's dream.

> *Following Bohm's theory, the mind contributes to the phenomenon of reality itself, not just to the knowledge of it. In a brain that operates holographically, the remembered image of a thing can have as much impact on the senses as the thing itself.[8]*

In other words, our imaginations have the same impact on the physical world as do objects, the things we believe are real. If we look at the universe as a holographic system, we realize that paranormal phenomena, Jung's "meaningful coincidences" or synchronicity, suggest that everything is connected.

Because of this connection, Monte, in 1990, applied these ideas to dreaming consciousness. His thinking was futuristic in that the concept of "unconditional love energy" so widely discussed today is embedded in his writings, his process, his teachings, and his philosophy:

> This implies and I believe correctly that consciousness, awake or dreaming, is contextual in nature and that we lose sight of this in our assumption that it is our unique gift to do with as we want. The capacity to love is the most coherent way of relating to the context. When that capacity is impaired, efforts at healing are set in motion in a way similar to the efforts at repair when our physical system is damaged in any way. It is in this sense that dreaming consciousness is a natural healing system. Healing occurs by exposing impediments to connectedness and the exploration of the coping resources available. Just as we are not in control of our own natural healing potential in response to trauma, infection or other sources of impairment, dreaming is an unconscious effort at healing, biologically enforced and spontaneously set in motion. The result is a deeper sense of connectivity to our own past and to others.[9]

As a psychiatrist, Monte was concerned with personal truth. He attempted to demystify the dream to "make the personal honesty embedded in the metaphorical images of our dreams available to all." We all have "an incorruptible core of being" that speaks our truth as well as society's truth:

> Our dreaming psyche arises out of an incorruptible core of our being that, in contrast to our waking ego, has never lost sight of the fact that we are members of a single species. Our ability to endure as a species may depend on taking that fact more seriously than we have in the past. Dreams reveal the state of connectedness of the individual to his or her past, to others, and to the supports and constraints of the social order. Is it too much to hope that, as we move into a postindustrial society, the intrinsic honesty of dreams can be harnessed to this effort?[10]

More recently, in 2007, Gregg Braden, in *The Divine Matrix*, has outlined in scientific terms how we are all connected. Braden applies theories in physics to the role of human consciousness as we access this quantum force to create our thoughts, feelings, emotions, and beliefs: "Both science and mysticism describe a force that connects everything together and gives us the power to influence how matter behaves—and reality itself—simply through the way we perceive the world around us."[11]

Indeed, Monte was ahead of his time. He knew that because we are all connected, we connect to the messages of one another's dreams. He knew his dream group process was based in science. The next chapter reminds us of the resources embedded in dreams: the solutions to problems and the creation of art, literature, and scientific discoveries.

7

Functions of Dreams

CREATIONS AND SOLUTIONS

Throughout the centuries, dreams have been an important part of life. Dreams have served multiple purposes, ranging from making predictions to solving problems to inspiring artworks. Deirdre Barrett, a clinical psychologist and professor at Harvard, conducts research on dreams and hypnosis. In *The Committee of Sleep*,[12] she describes how dreams have inspired contemporary artists, writers, filmmakers, musicians, scientists, and inventors across the globe—a worthwhile read.

HEALING

Healing is a focal point of the Ullman dream process. In most instances, the dreamer heals emotionally by learning what the sleeping mind is saying about waking life. People have changed their life courses from dream images—as in "The Orphan Dream" described in *Discover the Beliefs Hidden in Your Dreams*.[13]

Physical healing can also be a result of information from a dream. Often dreams warn the dreamer that something in the body needs attention, that something is out of balance. From this information, the dreamer can create imagery to aid the physical healing of disease. Tallulah Lyons has outlined how to do this in her book *Dreams and Guided Imagery: Gifts for Transforming Illness and Crisis*.[14] She worked with Wendy Pannier to create the Cancer Project for the IASD.

8

The Biology of Dreams

WHERE DO DREAMS ORIGINATE?

Hundreds of books explain the origin of dreams, how to manipulate them, and how to understand their meaning. Briefly, the mind processes previous events and feelings during the rapid eye movement (REM) phase of sleep. The dreamer's subconscious mind, during the REM phase, which occurs as often as every ninety minutes, conjures images as puns, double meanings, and metaphors based on the day's, week's, or month's concerns and feelings. It is the way a person thinks when she is asleep, free of the ego-driven filters of the conscious mind. When awake, a person edits and revises statements and appearances to save face in the waking world. However, the subconscious mind has no such need. It creates images of beliefs and feelings that most would prefer not to know themselves, much less present to the world. Exploring the messages of dreams challenges the waking conscious mind. Because the conscious mind wants to edit, it challenges us as soon as we attempt to capture dream images with words. Dream images seem to evaporate when we describe them.

Because of the waking mind's resistance to what the subconscious mind is saying in these metaphorical images, a dreamer can benefit from more input from sympathetic, caring listeners. Besides free association of the images, "the dreamer must zero in on the recent emotional soil in which the dream took root; explore the full range of associations that come to mind in connection with each image in the dream; and then work with the information now available to capture the metaphorical quality of the dream."[15] The metaphors contain the image with the associative data to enlighten current waking life circumstances.

Many people say, "But I don't dream. I can't remember my dreams." Nearly everyone dreams if he achieves REM sleep. Anyone who dreams is most likely to recall a dream if he sets the intention to do so before drifting off to sleep and records the dream immediately upon awakening. Because REM sleep typically occurs every ninety minutes, we dream all night long. Unless we awaken to record our dreams, they tend to evaporate.

According to Ullman, no one dreams of something she is unprepared to explore. Therefore even frightening dreams can be explored in a supportive environment in which the dream sharer determines the limits of exploration. A caveat is necessary, however: if nightmares are a result of an extremely distressing condition, such as post-traumatic stress disorder, a professional mental health worker should be consulted.

The Subconscious Mind

The subconscious mind exists to keep us safe. It controls heart rate, breathing rate, and hormone levels through the endocrine system. People don't consciously think, "Breathe in, breathe out." The subconscious does this automatically. This is how it works. The subconscious precipitates emotions, which trigger hormones to regulate heart and breathing rates to respond to danger. These parts are interactive. For example, if a person sees an oncoming car about to crash into him head-on, fear precipitates adrenalin and cortisone, which in turn increases the person's heart and breathing rates to prepare the muscles to react to avoid the crash. The body goes on high alert to keep the individual safe.

Additionally, the subconscious is a memory bank. It contains memories at conception, memories from ancestors, and memories from society. Remember Marilyn's dream? Ancestor beliefs and memories precipitated her annual August angst. Was the purpose to torture her? It certainly was torturing her, but her subconscious believed it was keeping her safe. Some of our beliefs and memories no longer serve us. Dream work is a way to begin to find these memories and beliefs to change them so they are updated and help us achieve more peaceful and joyful lives. This is what Monte was attempting to teach us with his Experiential Dream Group process.

9

A Memory of Monte

I participated in Monte's dream groups for about fifteen years. During this time, he was training us and sharing his past with us. He was an accomplished psychiatrist, neurologist, parapsychologist, researcher, and academician.

Sometimes when the group had extra time, Monte regaled us with stories of his paranormal interests, attempting to explain them through the current principles of quantum physics, which he had learned from personal conversations with David Bohm. Other times, he told us about his dream lab and the telepathic dream studies of the 1960s and 1970s. Over the years, the group gained much personal information and hard copies of his published articles. However, his most memorable stories were of his personal life.

Monte grew up in Washington Heights and on the Upper West Side of Manhattan with conservative parents who held high expectations for their children. Monte and his friends graduated from high school at fifteen and sixteen and enrolled in City College. One friend, Len, had read a lot about psychic phenomena after another friend, Gil, had described the poltergeist that had plagued his apartment. This entity threw hairpins at the walls and oatmeal over the carpet. Monte, fascinated and curious, joined his friends for séances to contact this entity.

From 1932 to 1934, a group of seven boys, sometimes with girlfriends, held regular Saturday night "sittings." The boys gathered in one apartment, darkened the room, and sat around a table with hands lightly touching on the tabletop. These "sitters" concentrated their energy and focused on raising the table. After a few sessions, the table tipped more and more and finally levitated so high that one member had to grab a leg. To make sure no one was lifting it, the boys switched from a bridge table to a forty- or fifty-pound table. Elated with the results, they pushed the envelope further by making psychic photos in 1933. They placed their hands and objects, such as keys and bottles, on top of a box containing a sealed, non-exposed plate. When they developed the plate in the bathroom, out came the objects as images on the plate!

Ever the explorers, they moved to thought photography. When a sitter visualized a page from a book, the image of a newspaper column appeared on the non-exposed plate; a picture of a girl's face in the mind of another sitter produced an "Indian idol." A stepsister of one of the sitters saw the photo of the "Indian idol," which reminded her of an object she had brought home from a trip out West. Despite searching everywhere, the object was not located until housecleaning the next spring: it was behind a book cabinet. Thrilling successes and invitations by respected psychic groups continued to excite and inspire them.

The group then decided to contact the "force" that appeared to be moving the table and making the photos. Their questions ready, the sitters gathered, concentrated their energy, and contacted the entity. Dr. Bindelof appeared. They received several messages from him over the next few years, which Monte, the group's secretary, carefully recorded. Years later, by his own admission, Monte did not want to publicize the Bindelof experience. As a Freudian-trained psychiatrist in the 1950s, Monte was establishing credibility with colleagues unlikely to be receptive to psi phenomena. The fear of ridicule prevailed. However, the desire to publish was never extinguished.

Monte gathered his compatriots for reunions in 1966, 1969, and 1971 to help recall these psi phenomena and to learn of the impact they had had on each of them. He collected written accounts and documents of the séances and taped interviews, intending to publish in the future. Yet this information rested in the closet as members of the Bindelof Sitters passed away one by one. Finally, in 2001, Monte published the accounts.

We, as members of his dream group, heard these fascinating tales in installments, not necessarily in chronological order. The vignettes came when we finished early with a dream, when we were having coffee and pastry during break, or just when Monte got the urge.

Not until after Monte had passed in June 2008 did I realize the extent to which the Bindelof experience had shaped his career. I dug into my files and read Monte's commemorative website.[16] He trained in neurology, psychiatry, and psychoanalysis and went into private practice from 1946 to 1974. During this time, he founded and directed the first community mental health center in New York City at Maimonides Medical Center. He also directed a sleep laboratory to study dreams and telepathy, which resulted in one of his books, *Dream Telepathy*.

In 1974, after many academic publications and years of serving as president of numerous professional organizations, Monte resigned from Maimonides Medical Center. This allowed him time to develop his ideas of his dream group process. Not only did he develop this very structured, safe approach to exploring dreams but he also trained people in his technique in the United States, Sweden, and Finland. As I looked back on the years of participation in Monte's dream groups, I realized I had not appreciated him for his innumerable accomplishments.

On one level, I knew he was an academic giant, but his demeanor, compassion, and healing statements made me realize he was a very able, ordinary giant—an ordinary giant, but elfish and with a sense of humor at the same time. Although small in stature, he let us know who was boss now and again to protect the psychological safety of the dreamer. At the beginning of each session, he told us who had "priority" because he kept track of who had shared dreams and on what dates. If two people wanted to share, he encouraged each person to explain the urgency of her dream. The dreamers themselves decided. This step allowed the dreamer to establish control, which enhanced safety. To further protect the sharing dreamer, Monte was quick to stop anyone from asking leading questions. When in doubt, I did not ask a question for fear of being called out. He reminded me of my father: better to be right than wrong! When no one responded to the question, "Who has a short, recent dream to share?" and someone squeaked, "I have a dream, but it's very small and not so important," Monte would say, "*There's no such thing as an unimportant dream*!" He was a friendly little giant!

After Monte's beloved wife, Janet, died in 2001, the dream group did not meet. Imagining the enormity of his grief, I wondered if Monte would ever resume the group. Finally I called him. He gave me the date of the next meeting. We group members approached his house with trepidation and were rather subdued as we entered Monte's living room. After we had settled into our usual seats, Monte inquired, as usual, "Who has a dream to share?"

No one responded. Total silence.

"Does anyone have a dream to share?" More silence.

"Well, if no one has a dream, I have one, but it's only a fragment."

At last! The group replied gently, "There's no such thing as a small, unimportant dream, Monte." The dream was a fragment, not even a whole sentence. We processed that fragment for nearly two hours. It was healing for Monte and the group. We now knew that the dream group would continue even though Janet was no longer on the earth.

Something important happened during that session: Monte revealed more of his vulnerabilities and his regrets, presenting himself as a "real" human, more than an academic who needed scientific proof to present to the world. It taught me that regardless of the public stature of the person, we meet on the level playing field of the dream world. He gave us a way to appreciate the messages from dream feelings and metaphors that promote personal growth and increase compassion. After all, how can you be angry with someone who shares a dream? That is Monte's true gift to the world—and to himself.

APPENDIX: DREAM GROUP PROCESS

Purpose	Skills Required	
• To help dreamer find meaning in a dream	**Listening**	**Questioning**
• Not therapy	• Take notes • Look at dreamer • No suggestions • No interruptions	• No leading questions • No information-demanding questions • No topics not initiated by dreamer
• Not counseling		

Volunteer a Dream	Stage I: The Dream	

• Leader asks who wishes to share a dream.
• If more than one dreamer volunteers, they discuss and decide among themselves.
	• Dreamer tells dream slowly; all record it verbatim.
	• Clarifying questions
	   o Who/what is real in waking life?
	   o Any colors in the dream?
	   o Descriptions without interpretations.
	   o Any feelings while dreaming?	

Stage II: The Game—Any participant volunteers; dreamer takes notes.	
A. Feelings • Use stem: "In my dream, I feel…" • Do not look at dreamer	**B. Metaphors** • Leader asks for metaphors. • Use stem: "In my version of the dream…" • Do not look at dreamer.

Stage III: Dreamer's Response and Dialogue		
A. Dreamer's Response: The dreamer responds to the group's projections for as long as she wishes without interruption.		
B1. Dialogue: Context • Open-ended questions about events prior to dream. • "Can you say anything more about…?"	**B2. Dialogue: Playback** • Member reads dream, scene by scene changing "I" to "you." • Dreamer responds at any time • "Can you say anything more about…?"	**B3. Dialogue: Orchestration** • Connections between images and dreamer's life that have not been stated. • Dreamer takes notes.
B4. Dialogue: Final Word The dreamer has the final word about the ideas and dream process.		
Stage IV: Delayed Orchestrations		
At the beginning of the following session, delayed insights can be given by the dreamer and group members.		

NOTES

1. Gardiner, *Ullman Legacy.*
2. Ullman, "Dreams and a New Politics of Connectedness."
3. Obon is an annual Buddhist event for commemorating one's ancestors. It is believed the ancestors' spirits return to this world to visit their relatives. See http://japan-guide.com/e/e2286.html.
4. Ullman, "Experiential Dream Group," 13–14.
5. Ibid.
6. Ullman et al., *Dream Telepathy.*
7. "Quantum Physics: David Bohm," http://www.spaceandmotion.com/Physics-David-Bohm-Holographic-Universe.htm.
8. Ibid.
9. Ullman, "Dreams, Species-Connectedness, and the Paranormal," 105–25.
10. Ullman, "Dreams and a New Politics of Connectedness," 275–76.
11. Braden, *Divine Matrix,* 79.
12. Barrett, *Committee of Sleep.*
13. Wahl, *Dream Digging.*
14. Lyons, *Dreams and Guided Imagery.*
15. Ullman, "Guidelines for Teaching Dreamwork."
16. http://siivola.org/.

BIBLIOGRAPHY

Barrett, Deirdre. *The Committee of Sleep: How Artists, Scientists, and Athletes Use Dreams for Creative Problem-Solving—and How You Can Too.* New York: Crown, 2010.

Braden, Gregg. *Divine Matrix: Bridging Time, Space, Miracles, and Belief.* Carlsbad, CA: Hay House, 2007.

Gardiner, Judy B. *The Ullman Legacy: Tributes: Guidelines for Montague Ullman's Dream Group Process and Its Derivatives.* 2009. http://www.siivola.org/.

Lyons, Tallulah. *Dreams and Guided Imagery: Gifts for Transforming Illness and Crisis.* Bloomington, IN: Balboa Press, 2012.

Ullman, Montague. *Appreciating Dreams: A Group Approach.* Thousand Oaks, CA: Sage, 1996.

———. "Dreams and a New Politics of Connectedness." In *Voices on the Threshold of Tomorrow: 145 Views of the New Millennium,* edited by Georg Feverstein and Trisha Lamb Feverstein, 275–76. Wheaton, IL: Quest Books, 1993.

———. "Dreams, Species-Connectedness, and the Paranormal." *Journal of the American Society of Psychical Research* 84 (1990): 105–25. http://siivola.org/monte/papers_grouped/uncopyrighted/Dreams/on_the_relevance_of_quantum_concepts_to_dreaming_consciousness.htm.

———. "The Experiential Dream Group." In *The Variety of Dream Experience: Expanding Our Ways of Working with Dreams,* edited by Montague Ullman and Claire Limmer, 13–19. Albany: State University of New York Press, 1999.

———. "Guidelines for Teaching Dreamwork." 1991. http://siivola.org/monte/papers_grouped/copyrighted/Dreams/Guidelines_for_Teaching_Dreamwork.htm.

Ullman, Montague, Stanley Krippner, and Alan Vaughan. *Dream Telepathy: Experiments in Noctural Extrasensory Perception.* Charlottesville, VA: Hampton Roads, 2001.

Wahl, Janet. *Discover the Hidden Beliefs in Your Dreams.* Albuquerque, NM: MindBalance LLC, forthcoming.

International Association for the Study of Dreams, http://www.asdreams.org/

Montague Ullman, collection of publications, http://siivola.org/monte/

About the Author

Janet Wahl, PhD, CHt, began her career as a teacher. After earning her PhD in Language, Literacy, and Learning, she served as a special education director and consultant, assistant professor, and assistant superintendent for curriculum and instruction. During fifteen years of that time, she participated in Montague Ullman's dream groups and took his leadership training workshops. After retirement, she studied hypnotherapy and ThetaHealing. As a ThetaHealing Master, she combined ThetaHealing techniques with dream work. She currently sees clients and teaches courses in dream work and ThetaHealing.

CPSIA information can be obtained at www.ICGtesting.com
Printed in the USA
BVOW02s1827021215

429169BV00004B/48/P